True Stories of Animal Heroes

Sterling

True Stories
of Animal Heroes

Sterling

Vita Murrow   Laivi Põder

Frances Lincoln
Children's Books

It was the time of disco, flower crowns, and spreading the love. The heartbeat of the era thumped from big cities to country fields. It reached all the way to Sterling the moose, who lived in a woodsy marsh.

Sterling was as tall as a truck and weighed 1,000 pounds. He was covered in thick brown hair and had a soft, shaggy beard. Trees brushed against the sturdy antlers on his head. And in Sterling's eyes was a twinkle, which hinted at something special in his heart . . . a love for cows.

Luckily for him, beside his marsh stood a grand dairy farm. It was home to a big herd of cows, and a busy farmer.

With their big brown eyes and square silhouette, Sterling was bewitched. But—*oh, no!*—the farmer had built a long fence that made sure the cows of the dairy farm never, ever crossed paths with the animals from the woodsy marsh.

Hmph! No farmer was going to keep Sterling from love. One day, while Sterling was working out some grass from his big ol' teeth and not looking where he was going, he backed up into the fence.

It creaked against his 1,000 pound weight.
Sterling had an idea. He squared up his rear and
with a *thump!* he pushed at the fence.

The fence gave way and Sterling had before him an opportunity. A whole field of cows...

Sterling bounded among them, sat down and winked his twinkling eyes.

The cows loved Sterling's groovy vibe!

Until the farm dog arrived and scurried them back to the barn.

The next day, Sterling came back to the broken fence to hang out with the cows. The farmer did not approve and sent farm dogs to draw the cows away. But Sterling followed.

The farmer roared the tractor to send Sterling away.
But Sterling charged past.

When the farmer fixed the fence, Sterling and the cows leaned on it with their united weight until it fell. Nothing could keep Sterling from his new friends.

Then one day Sterling could not see the cows anywhere. So, he followed the farmer. But it was a trick! Sterling followed the farmer right into a big trailer. Before he knew it, the gate was closed, and the trailer pulled out onto a road. The ride made him sleepy.

When Sterling woke, he found the farmer had dropped him at the Canadian border!

Alone in a new wilderness, Sterling hatched a plan. No farmer was going to keep him from finding love. Sterling had tricks of his own. His fluffy beard to the ground, he nosed along until he discovered tire tracks. He followed them along a country roadway, until he reached another dairy farm . . .

Sterling sniffed the air. When cows eat, they are gassy, and can let off up to 320 liters of gas a day. But Sterling didn't mind! He followed the smell toward a fenced field.

At that same moment, on the other side of the fence, a brown cow named Star was munching greens. Star thought the air around her was much too stinky. So, she backed farther and farther away from the herd.

Sterling lined his bum up to break this new fence. And at just the same time, Star's rump backed closer and closer to the fence until—*bump!*—the two rears collided.

The fence gave way, and with it, Sterling's heart.
It was all disco, and flower crowns and love.
The other cows crowded round, and Sterling
beckoned for them to follow him.

With a thunder of hooves Sterling led the cows through the broken fence, into the fields, and toward a new future.

The alarmed farmer was close behind, but the herd was Sterling's now. He gave the farmer a grin and his signature wink. The farmer was so unsettled that they scurried up the nearest tree.

From then on, nothing could stand in the way of a cow and a moose, ready to break down fences, let off gas, and spread the love.

Did you know this book is based on the real-life story of a moose in the United States?

In 1977, a 1,000-pound moose befriended cows on a dairy farm in Morrisville, USA. He threatened anyone who tried to milk them. The moose had to be moved to a wildlife sanctuary in Holland VT, which is beside the Canadian border into Quebec. But the determined guy escaped, and in protest set free a herd of cows from a nearby farm. When humans confronted him, the moose chased them up a tree! This is just one of many accounts of moose befriending cows. Stories have been recorded from the USA all the way to Germany.

Moose and cows have a lot in common. The names of their family members are the same: bull, cow, and calf for their little ones. Moose and cows both eat mostly plants in multi-chambered stomachs. And of course, they both let off a lot of gas.

Humans have a close relationship with cows; we raise them for food and milk, and cows are a part of religious devotion for many. Moose are less close to humans. We hunt them, use their habitat, leave behind chemicals, and cause accidental fires, which make it hard for moose to thrive. You can be a moose ally by learning ways to safeguard their future, so they can continue to make new friends.

www.iucn.org

ℭHE MESMERIZED MOOSE *"I don't want no sideshow," said Larry Carrara. But that's what he got.*

IT BEGAN IN October 1986, when Larry Carrara of Shrewsbury, Vermont, who worked at the General Electric plant in North Claremont and did a little farming up on Carrara Mountain, saw a 700-pound bull moose in one of his pastures. The moose seemed mesmerized by Jessica, one of Larry's Hereford cows and stared at her for days before beginning a more active courtship. He stood next to Jessica, nuzzling her and pushing other cows away when Larry or his wife, Lila, brought out the feed. Wildlife experts said it was not unusual for a rutting male moose to fix his attention on a cow or mare — in a week or two, when

The lovelorn moose Carrara called Josh paid court to Jessica the cow for 76 days.

Moose-match

the mating season ended, he'd come to his senses and be on his way.

But it would be 76 days before the moose left, and by that time some 75,000 people had come to Carrara Mountain to see the mismatched pair. A team of Nashville songwriters penned a ballad called "Lovesick Moose" that got wide airplay. Environmentalists attempted to adopt the moose as a symbol of their efforts to prevent expansion of a nearby ski area. A justice of the peace running for the state legislature came to the farm to perform a marriage ceremony for the moose and cow, but was turned away by Larry. "I don't want no sideshow," he said.

Then on January 7, 1987, the moose, which Larry had taken to calling Josh, lost one of his antlers — a normal winter development than biologists say reduces a male moose's nat-

Larry recalls, "and I told my wife, 'He's going to leave tomorrow.' The next day he was gone."

Larry is on disability retirement from GE now, and Lila runs Carrara Mountain Country Store, where tourists still stop by to talk about Jessica and Josh, buy T-shirts, or get autographed copies of *A Moose for Jessica,* the book Larry wrote about the rural romance. Larry gets letters every week from children who have read his book; he's thinking maybe he should take them to his publisher to see if there's any interest in a sequel. Jessica is 12 years old — middle-aged, for a cow — and doing fine. As for Josh, the lovelorn moose, Larry thinks he may have come back one more time, in May 1987. "I saw this moose standing in the woods, looking into the pasture, where I had a couple of horses at the time. I got my camera and walked up to this moose, talking to him, trying to get close enough to see the inverted-V-shaped scar Josh had over his right eye. But the horses ran up to me and scared him away. I haven't seen him since."

— TIM CLARK

Brimming with creative inspiration, how-to projects, and useful information to enrich your everyday life, Quarto Knows is a favourite destination for those pursuing their interests and passions. Visit our site and dig deeper with our books into your area of interest: Quarto Creates, Quarto Cooks, Quarto Homes, Quarto Lives, Quarto Drives, Quarto Explores, Quarto Gifts, or Quarto Kids.

Text © 2021 Vita Murrow. Illustrations © 2021 Laivi Põder
First published in the US in 2021 by Frances Lincoln Children's Books,
an imprint of The Quarto Group.
100 Cummings Center, Suite 265D, Beverly, MA 01915, USA.
T +1 978-282-9590 F +1 078-283-2742 www.QuartoKnows.com

ISBN 978-0-7112-6399-4
Published by Katie Cotton
Designed by Karissa Santos
Edited by Katy Flint
Production by Dawn Cameron
Manufactured in Guangdong, China TT052021
9 8 7 6 5 4 3 2 1

Photo Credits p29: Clockwise from left: Evening Panorama in Rural New York State, via Getty; Bullwinkle the moose rests his head on Jessica the cow during their 'romance' in Shrewsbury, Vt., in this Dec. 1986 file photo. © AP Photo/ Toby Talbot; Bullwinkle the moose rests his head on Jessica the cow in a pasture in Shrewsbury in this photo from Nov. 7, 1986 © AP Photo via Shutterstock; From "The Mesmerized Moose" Yankee Magazine, April 1994.

MIX
Paper from
responsible sources
FSC® C016973
FSC
www.fsc.org

Also in the **True Stories of Animal Heroes** series:

FLUFFLES
978-0-7112-6159-4

ONYX
978-0-7112-6145-7

STERLING
978-0-7112-6399-4

TALALA
978-0-7112-6395-6